Carnivore Diet

*Easy Meat Based Recipes
for Natural Weight Loss*

Carnivore Cookbook for Beginners with 2 Weeks Meal Plan to Reset &
Energize Your Body

Kaitlyn Donnelly

Disclaimer

The recipes and information in this book are provided for educational purposes only. Please always consult a licensed professional before making changes to your lifestyle or diet. The author and publisher shall have neither liability nor responsibility to anyone with respect to any loss or damage caused or alleged to be caused directly or indirectly by the information contained in this book. All trademarks and brands within this book are for clarifying purposes only and are owned by the owners themselves, not affiliated with this document.

Images from shutterstock.com

CONTENTS

INTRODUCTION

There is a new diet trend of that has attracted the attention of the masses. The carnivore diet completely contradicts the dietary tips we have been taught before. Of all the trends, this diet is the most extreme.

The carnivore diet has been around for thousands of years. Our ancestors adhered strictly to animal-based diets, and some of our longest-lived populations flourished as carnivores long before "dietary trends" were brought to life. The carnivore diet is trendy for a good reason.

The carnivore diet is simple: you eat only animal meat for all your nutritional needs. It is a zero carb diet and classified as a high protein diet

There are no vegetables or fruit, or any processed carbohydrates like grains and cereals.

A strict follower will eat only meat and drink only water. Whereas others may include drinks like tea and coffee, or other sources of fat like dairy products.

CHAPTER 1. A Beginner's Guide to an All-Meat Diet

What is the Carnivore Diet?

The carnivore diet is easy to follow: you only eat animal products and foods. That means no vegetables, no fruits, and especially no carbs. This is almost the complete opposite of a vegan diet.

Although this may seem crazy at first, many people theorize that plant-based food is not required to live. Actually, carbohydrates – which can be found in plants – are the only insignificant macronutrient. This means proteins and fats are necessary for our body to thrive, but we can get them without consuming any carbohydrates.

The carnivorous diet consists of these zero carb foods:

- Meat
- Cheese
- Butter
- Eggs

You don't have to count calories, come up with food timing strategies, or control your portion sizes.

Bottom line: to successfully adhere to the carnivorous diet, eat only animal products, and avoid everything else.

> *The carnivore diet is centered around one simple equation:*
>
> **Meat + Water = Health**

Getting Started – 5 Basic Rules

The best way to start is to do a 30-day challenge.

Use this time to see if you are subjectively feeling better (less pain and aches, better energy levels, less hunger, better sleep), or if you can see better physical health changes (weight loss, better thyroid levels, lower A1c levels).

Before and after photography, keeping a health diary, and tracking lab results will help you find out if this diet plan is for you.

By following the five rules below, you will get an excellent baseline for starting your own carnivore diet experiment.

1. What to Eat

You will not be eating plant-based proteins like pea or soy protein. The suggested types of meat you can eat will be any type of animal-based protein.

Recommended carnivore diet foods:

- Red Meat: beef, pork, lamb, wild game, birds.
- White Meat: chicken, turkey, fish, seafood.
- Organ Meat: liver, kidneys, tongue, bone marrow, heart, brain.
- Eggs: chicken eggs, goose eggs, duck eggs.
- Dairy: heavy cream, cheese, butter, ghee

Eat the fatty cuts of meat, not just lean cuts.

Fat on the meat provides additional daily nutritional needs that your body needs to maintain health; along with the vitamins, minerals, protein, and other nutrients you get from meat. Plus, fat makes any food tastier.

Here is a list of carnivore-approved foods:

- **Meat.** Your primary source of calories should come from fatty pieces of grass-fed meat like porterhouse, NY strip steak, ribeye, 80/20 ground beef, bacon, t-bone, flank steak, and pork chops. Since you restrict carbohydrates, meat with more fat is preferred so your body can use these fats as an energy source.
- **Fish.** Salmon, trout, sardines, catfish, and mackerel are allowed. Just like meat, focus on the fattiest fish you can buy.
- **Eggs.** Also known as a natural multivitamin, eggs are the perfect ratio of fats, proteins, and essential nutrients to support your body.
- **Bone Marrow**. Bone broth and marrow are carnivore-approved, and they are a great protein source that also help with skin, gut, and joint health.
- **Dairy**. Grass-fed butter, cheese, and milk are allowed because they come from an animal, but many carnivore dieters try to minimize milk consumption because of lactose intolerance.
- **Fatty meat food products**. Instead of vegetable oil, use tallow, lard, and other animal-based fats when cooking.
- **Condiments.** Salt, pepper, spices, and herbs are allowed. Stick to simple ingredients that contain neither sugar nor carbohydrates. If you want a little flavor with meat, consider adding a little hot sauce with zero calories.

2. How Much to Eat

You will want to eat until you feel full. If you have an insatiable hunger, you may not be eating enough fat. Try to eat fat first, then add meat.

Eat according to your energy needs. Many people eat an average of about 2 pounds of meat per day. However, if you workout out heavily, you might eat about 4 pounds of meat per day.

3. When to Eat

You can practice intermittent fasting or eat three meals a day.

It depends on your daily routine and on whether you want to add more health benefits, such as timed fasting. If you follow circadian biological thinking, then protein in the morning during the first hour after waking up helps set your body's clock. If you follow the advice of protein researcher Professor Stuart Phillips, then eating protein during the day and evening helps maintain muscle mass.

Eat when you are hungry. Over time, you will probably find that you only need 1-2 meals a day. But experiment with this later.

However, I am also a fan of intermittent fasting. In addition to reducing insulin (which you already do in this diet), it regulates mTOR activates and the AMPK pathway.

Intermittent fasting is something that you can experiment with after transitioning a carnivorous diet.

My schedule is the following:

- Eat for 8 hours a day
- Fast for 16 hours a day

4. How to Cook Your Meat

On the carnivore diet (zero carb diet), you can cook meat the way you like.

High-quality steak restaurants that value good tasting food cook red meat, like beef, to be medium-rare and not well-done. If you don't like steak that is slightly bloody or still pink; you might find that your tastes will change over time if you eat meat every day. Most likely, you will begin to enjoy eating medium-rare steak against well-done steak.

Cook other meat (fish, bacon, chicken) so that it is safe to eat. For example, do not eat raw bacon or raw chicken in terms of food safety. However, raw seafood is a must-try like salmon sushi, fresh oysters, or sashimi tuna.

There are many variants for how to cook meat. Prepare for your own taste.

But you have to make sure that you cook so that the meat is safe to eat, but also do not overcook the meat.

You can reduce the nutrient content of the following if the food is overcooked:

- Minerals: potassium, calcium magnesium, and sodium
- Water-soluble vitamins: B vitamins and vitamin C
- Fat soluble vitamins: vitamins A, D, E, and K

5. What to Drink

Most people drink only water in the first 30 days. It can be spring water, mineral water, ordinary tap water, or filtered water. Try adding a little sea salt to the water for extra electrolytes.

You can drink coffee or tea, as long as you do not add sugar or sweeteners. Avoid any hot or cold carbohydrate drinks like vegetable drinks, soda, energy drinks, shakes, protein powder, etc.

CARNIVORE DIET

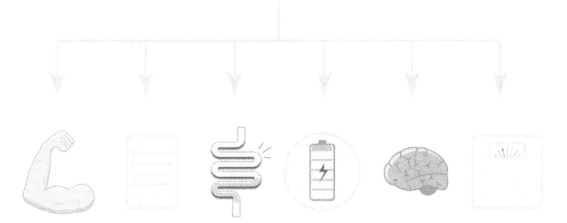

Benefits of the Carnivore Diet

The shocking number of anecdotal reports showing how beneficial a carnivorous diet can be to one's health is the reason why the all-meat diet has been brought to light. These benefits include:

Weight Loss

As a ketogenic diet, eating a strictly all-meat diet can help you lose weight faster and more efficiently than any other diet. By eating only animal fats and proteins, you move your main energy source from carbohydrates to fats.

When you are fat-adapted - also known as being in ketosis - your metabolism can use both stored and dietary body fat for fuel. It means you can burn off your own fat and use it as energy.

Protein and fat are very satiating. Studies have also shown that adapting fat improves hunger hormones, further regulating appetite.

Decreased Inflammation

Inflammation can be exacerbated by eating foods rich in carbohydrates. Processed foods, vegetable oils, and even some plant nutrients are associated with increased inflammatory reactions in the body.

Less inflammation through the carnivorous diet leads to less pains and aches. Additional collagen from protein sources will improve cartilage health, too.

Increased Testosterone

Healthy fats are in charge for optimal hormonal function, including testosterone. High-healthy-fat diets have been shown to improve testosterone levels.

Since you're consuming large amounts of healthy protein and fats on the carnivore diet, expect to see an increase in energy, muscle mass, and strength. And if you are a woman, don't worry. The increased fat will control your hormones.

Mental Clarity

Many carnivores have reported increased mental clarity, focus, and energy. This is likely due to running on ketones (fats) for energy, restriction of carbohydrates, and becoming fat-adapted.

Studies have shown that the brain prefers fats for energy over carbs.

Less Digestive Issues

It is believed that fiber is crucial to digestion. But people who adhere to the carnivorous diet believe in the opposite, with the science to back it up.

A 2012 study found that reducing the intake of fiber in people with chronic constipation significantly improved their symptoms, including strain, gas, and bloating. The group that ate a lot of fiber did not see any change in the symptoms of constipation.

List of Where to Buy Meat

- Local butcher shop (great place to learn and discuss anything meat)
- Local grocery store of supermarket
- Local farmers market (great place to meet the farmer and ask questions)
- Order meat online with home delivery

Useful Tips:

- Drinking enough water – drink to avoid dehydration and satisfy thirst
- Not eating too little food – it causes unwanted excessive weight loss
- Adding salt to food
- Not avoiding fatty meats – don't be afraid of cholesterol, it's good for you

What to Avoid?

Avoid the following foods:
- **Vegetables:** cauliflower, broccoli, potatoes, peppers, green beans, etc.
- **Fruits:** berries, apples, bananas, oranges, kiwi, etc.
- **High-lactose dairy:** yogurt, milk, soft cheese, etc.
- **Legumes:** beans, lentils, etc.
- **Nuts and seeds:** pumpkin seeds, almonds, pistachios, sunflower seeds, etc.
- **Grains:** rice, quinoa, wheat, bread, pasta, etc.
- **Alcohol:** wine, beer, liquor, etc.
- **Sugars:** maple syrup, table sugar, brown sugar, etc.
- **Beverages other than water:** soda, fruit juice, etc.
- **In the beginning, don't eat chicken.** The nutrient profile and fat is inferior to the other meats
- **Processed meats:** they contain too many additives. Look out for nitrites and nitrates, and avoid them.
- **Vegetable oils.**
- **Carbohydrates.**
- **Sauces.**
- **Supplements.**
- **Dark chocolate.**

Frequently Asked Questions

"Do I Only Have to Eat Grass-Fed Meat?"

No, there is no problem with eating meat that is not expensive and fits within your monthly budget available.

"Can I Eat Processed Meats?"

Processed cold meats like salami, ham, pepperoni, and chorizo are best avoided in the first 30 days if feasible. This is because these meats contain fillers with extra carbohydrates. Chomps – not your typical meat stick – is the best meat with simple spices. Chomps do not contain any preservatives or artificial ingredients, is made with grass-fed, free-range, and antibiotic/hormone-free proteins.

"Are Bacon and Sausages Okay to Eat?"

Yes and no. Bacon is great to eat, however, some sausages contain ingredients such as wheat to help fill them out. So be sure to read the nutrition label.

"Is This a Short-Term or Long-Term Diet?"

It can be used for both. You will find people in the zero carb diet community forums who have been eating a meat-only diet for several decades with no negative health effects reported by them.

"What About the Risk of Constipation?"

You will have regular bowel movements with fewer stools per day. This is because meat is more easily broken down and absorbed in the intestines, and thus, the yield is lower compared to a diet with a high content of insoluble fiber.

"Will Eating Too Much Meat Damage my Kidney?"

No. In fact, the opposite can happen, and kidney function can improve if you remove excess glucose from your diet and increase insulin sensitivity.

"Do I Have To Take Supplements?"

As a rule, no. But some people find it beneficial to take a potassium or magnesium supplement. Even on a meat-only diet, you should count on getting enough vitamin C. Strict carnivore eaters feel that if you eat the right types of meat and enough of them, it should provide all your necessary mineral and vitamin needs.

"Will I have any nutrient deficiency?"

The short answer is most likely No. Red meat contains just about every mineral and vitamin your body needs to live, including zinc, iron, selenium, vitamin D, vitamin B, protein, and more.

"Will it work for athletes?"

Yes. A lot of fitness enthusiasts assume that glucose from carbohydrates is the best source for immediate and quick energy to fuel competitions and workouts. On the carnivore diet, your body undergoes a process called gluconeogenesis, where some protein is converted to enough glucose for certain body functions.

"How long is the adaptation period?"

Around one month. You will be eating carbs all your life if you are like most other people. It takes time for your body to adjust to using fats and proteins as its primary source of energy.

"No vegetables? Really?"

Despite being told over and over when you were a kid, vegetables may not be as important as we thought. They certainly have nutrients and vitamins, but they may not be the best source.

ed meat bad for you?"

lot of things in life and nutrition, you have to look at the other variables at play. If you do not
e and eat a ton of red meat and sugar, you probably will not be very healthy. But if you exercise,
eat red meat, and avoid sugar, you will probably be in good shape.

"What about your cholesterol?"

There is a debate that meat or fat causes high cholesterol. There are a lot of variables that influence
cholesterol, and everything in our bodies for that matter. If you eat a lot of fat and sugar, it is completely
different from eating a lot of fat without sugar. It can be sugar that causes problems, not fat. Correlation
does not equal causality. Exercise is another important factor.

"What About Tea and Coffee?"

Some carnivores still drink coffee, but both coffee and tea have shown to cause some gut and
inflammation permeability issues. However, some people have a crippling addiction to coffee. If it's you,
don't cut it out at first. This will obscure the results of the carnivorous transition. If you believe you can
go a week without tea and coffee without breaking your boss's head, try slowing consumption and
transitioning out. Especially if there is something specific you're trying to treat.

"Dairy and Eggs?"

Both dairy and eggs can be inflammatory for some people. But you know your body best. So it's up to you.

Egg whites contain protective proteins that can cause acne, irritate the gut, and trigger autoimmune
disease. Egg white is actually one of the most common allergies, affecting about 1-3% of the population.

When I eat eggs, I filter the yolk and eat it myself. The yolk is much more nutritious. And the funniest
part is that it's the exact opposite of what most people are trying to do.

Dairy products can cause inflammation for two reasons: dairy proteins and lactose. If you just do not
tolerate lactose, you can try fermented foods and hard cheeses that have lactose fermented away. If it still
annoys you, then you should completely give up dairy, as these are probably proteins that bother you.

In the first 15-30 days of the carnivorous diet, given how often eggs and thrush cause inflammation, you
should also not eat. If you're feeling great after the first month, then experiment with adding them back.

How to Survive the First Month

The carnivore diet – also identified as the carnivorous diet or the all-meat diet– entails eating almost
nothing but meat for every meal and every day. This means a lot of fat, a lot of protein, and almost zero
carbs.

This is contrary to generally accepted dietary standards, such as "you need to eat a lot of grains,
vegetables, and fiber" which has contributed to the propagation of vegetarian and vegan diets. You'd
probably, expect the carnivore diet to cause weight gain, high cholesterol, digestive problems, and other
problems.

However, conventional wisdom is not always completely accurate.

The all-meat diet is based on the theory that our ancestors ate meat predominantly because it was
inefficient to collect a lot of vegetables or fruits. As a result, our bodies have developed to work optimally
on a meat-oriented diet. So the theory goes.

It was difficult for me to realize the notion that the carnivorous diet could not only not cause harm, but
truly improve my health. However, after seeing how people are sharing the positives they have achieved

I decided to experiment to see if it would really work for me. And because I love the taste of eating meat, it seemed like an all-meat diet that could be sustainable.

Before diving into the carnivore diet, it is important to know that the first month, and especially the first week, will be the most difficult.

You will face a few challenges when starting the carnivore diet. Let's discuss four of those challenges and how to overcome them.

1. Consult your doctor or nutritionist before trying. **Have a blood test** before starting and again 2-3 months after being on the carnivore diet. Everyone has different needs for metabolism, so it is important to know if your diet works with your body.
2. **The first week is the hardest**. Expect variations in your energy, appetite, and focus. Start on a week when you're not too busy.
3. **Be prepared for fluctuations in your appetite**. Your appetite may level out after the first few weeks once you will have found the right portion sizes to eat through the day. Be sure you have access to carnivore friendly food through the day until then. You will have some days when you want to eat without stopping and other days when you will not even think about food. Your appetite will adjust as soon as your body gets used to this diet.
4. **Do not give up when you are not feeling well**. You are more than likely to experience fatigue, headaches, and other flu-like symptoms during the first week of your diet. This is normal because your body is used to using fats to produce energy rather than carbohydrates.

Carnivore Diet Meal Plan Example

Getting started with a carnivorous diet is extremely easy. Here is an example of what a carnivorous diet looks like all day long.

- Breakfast – Eggs, bacon, water, black coffee
- Lunch – Salmon, water
- Dinner –NY strip steak with grass-fed butter, water
- Snack – Chomps, pork rinds, or bone broth, water

It doesn't get much easier, and you don't need to over-complicate it. In fact, if you like steak, you can eat it for breakfast, lunch, and dinner!

The Carnivore Diet is Worth Thinking

Although the trend towards meat consumption is still extremely new, our ancestors, hundreds of years ago, adhered to a similar food protocol, some of which lived to 100 years old.

With the amazing number of carnivores revitalizing their health – and the studies that support them – the carnivore diet will continue to gain popularity. If you would try this on your own, consult your doctor first and then follow the tips in this book.

BREAKFAST   LUNCH   DINNER

CHAPTER 2. Carnivore Diet Meal Plan and 5-Day Menu

Now about the interesting things. What does a week of eating all-meat really look like?

The goal of this plan is to transition you from a greater variety of meat to less. But still cut out the inflammatory food.

Week 1 Meal Plan

This week is an adaptation period. You'll be:

- Eating more pork and seafood
- Eating less beef
- Not eating bone marrow or organ meats

	Breakfast	**Lunch**	**Dinner**
Day 1	Lemon Baked Salmon (p.52)	Marinated Grilled Flank Steak (p.20)	Slow Cooker Pork (p.21)
Day 2	Easy Blackened Shrimp (p.53)	Pan-Fried Pork Tenderloin (p. 23)	Bangin' Coconut-Lime Skirt Steak (p.26)
Day 3	The Best Garlic Cilantro Salmon (p.55)	Grilled Lamb Chops (p.22)	Herb and Garlic Bison Roast Rib (p.27)
Day 4	Crispy Oven Roasted Salmon (p.56)	Pressure Cooker Pork Loin Roast (p.24)	Ribeye Steak Sauté (p.28)
Day 5	Aromatic Dover Sole Fillets (p.57)	Steak Au Poivre (p.29)	Pan-Fried Pork Tenderloin (p.23)
Day 6	Bacon-Wrapped Salmon (p.58)	Slow Cooker Pork (p.21)	Skillet Rib Eye Steaks (p.31)
Day 7	Garlic Ghee Pan-Fried Cod (p.60)	Ribeye Steak Sauté (p.28)	Slow Cooker Pork (p.21)

Week 2 Meal Plan

Week 2 is a transition to a steady-state diet. You'll be adding organ meats and bone marrow great source of DHA and fat (omega 3).

	Breakfast	**Lunch**	**Dinner**
Day 1	Steam Your Own Lobster (p.61)	Marinated Grilled Flank Steak (p.20)	Slow Cooker Pork (p.21)+Pan Seared Beef Tongue (p.65)
Day 2	Lemon Ghee Roast Chicken (p.44)	Pan-Fried Pork Tenderloin (p.23) +Beef Heart Steak(p. 67)	Bangin' Coconut-Lime Skirt Steak (p.26)
Day 3	The Best Garlic Cilantro Salmon (p.55)	Grilled Lamb Chops (p. 22)+ Slow Cooked Chicken Gizzard (p.68)	Herb and Garlic Bison Roast Rib (p.27)
Day 4	Pan-Fried Tilapia (p.63)	Asian Chicken Wings (p.39)	Ribeye Steak Sauté (p.28)+ Liver Bacon Meatballs(p.66)
Day 5	Aromatic Dover Sole Fillets (p.57)	Steak Au Poivre (p. 29)+Grilled Beef Liver Steak (p.69)	Pan-Fried Pork Tenderloin (p.23)
Day 6	Crispy Chicken Thighs (p.41)	Slow Cooker Pork (p.21)	Turkey Scotch Eggs (p.50)
Day 7	Roasted Paprica Turkey Wings (p.51)	Whole Roast Chicken (p.47)	Slow Cooker Pork (p.21)+ BBQ Chicken Livers (p.72)

Sample menu

Here is a 5-day sample menu for the carnivore diet:

Day 1

Breakfast: eggs, bacon, Lemon Baked Salmon

Lunch: salmon jerky, turkey burger patty, beef tips

Dinner: crab, filet mignon, chicken liver

Snacks: jerky, a small amount of Parmesan cheese

Day 2

Breakfast: eggs, shrimp, a glass of heavy cream

Lunch: tuna fish, strip steak, beef jerky

Dinner: scallops, lamb chops, beef liver

Snacks: bone broth, a small amount of Cheddar cheese

Day 3

Breakfast: eggs, turkey sausage, salmon

Lunch: pork chops,beef tips, mackerel

Dinner: a small amount of Parmesan cheese, turkey burger patty, bone marrow

Snacks: shrimp, hard-boiled eggs

Day 4

Breakfast: shredded chicken, trout, bacon

Lunch: a small amount of Cheddar cheese, beef meatballs, salmon jerky

Dinner: filet mignon, crab cooked in lard

Snacks: beef jerky, sardines

Day 5

Breakfast: eggs, turkey and chicken sausage links

Lunch: chicken liver, lamb roast, pork chop

Dinner: scallops cooked in butter, flank steak, a small glass of heavy cream

Snacks: turkey jerky, bone broth

CHAPTER 3. Recipes
RED MEAT

Italian Burgers

Prep time: 15 minutes (+6 hours)

Cooking time: none

Servings: 6-8

Nutrients per serving:

Carbohydrates – 10.4 g

Fat – 53.4 g

Protein – 47.6 g

Calories – 716

Ingredients:

- 1 lb grass-fed ground beef
- 2 tbsp Italian seasoning
- 2 tbsp garlic powder
- 1 tbsp onion powder
- ¼ cup coconut oil

Instructions:

1. Mix all ingredients and form burger patties from the mixture.
2. Pan-fry in coconut oil until done to your liking.

Marinated Grilled Flank Steak

Prep time: 8 hours

Cooking time: 30 minutes

Servings: 4

Nutrients per serving:

Carbohydrates – 15.2 g

Fat – 87.3 g

Protein – 95.2 g

Calories – 1241

Ingredients:

- 3 lbs flank steak, cut into long slices
- Marinade:
- 1 cup olive oil
- ⅔ cup coconut aminos
- ½ cup apple cider vinegar
- Juice of 1 lemon
- 2 tbsp mustard
- 6 cloves of garlic, crushed
- 1 tbsp grated fresh ginger
- 1 tbsp paprika
- 1 tbsp onion powder
- 1 tbsp salt
- 1 tsp chili powder
- 2 tsp dried thyme

Instructions:

1. Mix together all marinade ingredients.
2. Place steak into two ziplock bags and divide the marinade equally between the bags.
3. Seal the bags and marinate in the refrigerator at least 8 hours, or overnight.
4. Grill steak to your desired doneness.

Slow Cooker Pork

Prep time: 5 minutes

Cooking time: 8 hours

Servings: 4

Nutrients per serving:

Carbohydrates – 5.5 g

Fat – 28.2 g

Protein – 40.4 g

Calories – 423

Ingredients:

- 2 lb pork shoulder
- 1 tbsp salt
- 1 tbsp ginger powder
- 1 tbsp Szechuan peppercorns

Instructions:

1. Place pork shoulder in the slow cooker.
2. Top pork with the spices.
3. Set the slow cooker on low heat for 8 hours.
4. Turn the meat over after 6 hours but do not pull apart meat.

Grilled Lamb Chops

Prep time: 10 minutes

Cooking time: 8 minutes

Servings: 8

Nutrients per serving:

Carbohydrates – 0.5 g

Fat – 34 g

Protein – 83 g

Calories – 665

Ingredients:

- 8 lamb chops, 1¼ inch thick

Marinade:

- 3 tbsps olive oil
- 2 tbsps fresh rosemary, chopped
- 3 cloves garlic, minced
- ½ tsp freshly ground black pepper
- 1 tsp kosher salt

Instructions:

1. Preheat the grill to medium-high.
2. Place lamb chops on a plate in a single layer.
3. In a small bowl, mix all marinade ingredients and spoon evenly over both sides of lamb chops.
4. Grill chops to the desired doneness.
5. Transfer to a platter and let rest for 10 minutes before serving.

Recipe Notes:

If you'd like to cook on the stovetop, preheat a grill pan over medium-high and cook as on the grill.

Pan-Fried Pork Tenderloin

ep time: 5 minutes

oking time: 20 minutes

rvings: 2

Nutrients per serving:

rbohydrates – 0 g

t – 15 g

otein – 47 g

lories – 330

Ingredients:

- 1 lb pork tenderloin
- 1 tbsp coconut oil
- Salt and pepper, to taste

Instructions:

1. Cut the pork tenderloin in half.
2. In a frying pan over medium heat, add the coconut oil.
3. Once the coconut oil melts, place the pork halves into the frying pan.
4. Cook all sides until the meat thermometer shows an internal temperature of just below 145°F. The pork will continue cooking a bit after you take it out of the pan.
5. Let the pork sit 5 minutes and then slice into 1-inch thick slices.

Pressure Cooker Pork Loin Roast

Prep time: 10 minutes

Cooking time: 35 minutes

Servings: 9

Nutrients per serving:

Carbohydrates – 1.1g

Fat – 11.5 g

Protein – 29.2 g

Calories – 228

Ingredients:

- 3 lb pork loin roast
- 1 tsp dried oregano
- 1 tsp onion powder
- 1 tsp ground cumin
- 1 tsp garlic powder
- 1 tsp coriander
- 1 tsp dried thyme
- 1 tbsp olive oil
- ½ tsp salt
- 2 cloves garlic, minced
- 2 cups chicken bone broth

Instructions:

1. Mix garlic powder, onion powder, coriander, oregano, salt, cumin, and thyme in a small bowl. Rub mixture into pork.
2. Heat oil in the pressure cooker on sauté, then stir fry minced garlic until fragrant.
3. Add pork and brown all sides.
4. Remove pork and deglaze the pot with one cup of bone broth.
5. Add the remaining broth, then place rack in the bottom of the pot. Put the pork roast on top of the rack.
6. Cook on high for 25 minutes. When done, do a quick pressure release.
7. Remove roast from the pot and let sit for 10-15 minutes before slicing.

Prosciutto-Wrapped Whole Roasted Beef Tenderloin

Prep time: 20 minutes

Cooking time: 26-28 minutes

Servings: 10-12

Nutrients per serving:

Carbohydrates – 0.2 g

Fat – 15.5 g

Protein – 39.2 g

Calories – 300

Ingredients:

- 4 lbs trimmed whole beef tenderloin
- 4 oz deli sliced prosciutto
- 1 tbsp chopped garlic
- 1 tbsp olive oil
- 1 tbsp fresh parsley, chopped
- 1 tbsp kosher salt
- ¼ tsp ground black pepper

Instructions:

1. Preheat the oven to 425° F
2. In a small bowl, combine the olive oil, garlic, salt, fresh parsley, and pepper.
3. Rub the mixture into the tenderloin.
4. Gently wrap the beef tenderloin in overlapping ribbons of prosciutto until covered.

5. Place the tenderloin on a cookie sheet and roast to desired doneness.
6. Remove from the oven and allow to rest about 10-15 minutes before slicing.

Recipe Notes:

Please remember that these times for roasting are a general guideline because the thickness of the tenderloin and ovens can vary – it's always best to check it with a meat thermometer to be sure it's done the way you want.

Bangin' Coconut-Lime Skirt Steak

Prep time: 10 minutes (+20 minutes)

Cooking time: 30 minutes

Servings: 4

Nutrients per serving:

Carbohydrates – 2.6 g

Fat – 57.2 g

Protein – 46.1 g

Calories – 702

Ingredients:

- 2 lbs grass-fed skirt steak
- ½ cup coconut oil, melted
- Juice and zest of one lime
- 1 tbsp minced garlic
- 1 tsp grated fresh ginger
- 1 tsp red pepper flakes
- ¾ tsp sea salt
- 2 sprigs fresh parsley, chopped

Instructions:

1. In a large bowl, mix the garlic, coconut oil, lime juice and zest, ginger, salt, and red pepper flakes.
2. Add steak to the marinade and toss to coat.
3. Allow meat to marinate for about 20 minutes at room temperature.
4. Place steak and marinade in a large skillet over medium-high heat.
5. Cook steak to your desired doneness.

Herb and Garlic Bison Roast Rib

Prep time: 10 minutes (+8 hours)

Cooking time: 50 minutes

Servings: 6

Nutrients per serving:

Carbohydrates – 1 g

Fat – 19.2 g

Protein – 33.5 g

Calories – 328

Ingredients:

- 2½ lbs bison roast rib
- 1 tsp olive oil
- 4 cloves fresh garlic, minced
- 1 tsp thyme
- 1 tsp oregano
- ½ tsp sage
- Sea salt, to taste
- 1 cup hot water

Instructions:

1. In a small bowl, mix the oregano, minced garlic, thyme, oil, and sage.
2. Rub mixture into roast rib. Allow to sit for 8 hours or overnight in the fridge.
3. Remove roast rib 30 minutes before putting it in the oven.
4. Preheat the oven to 500°F.
5. Place the roast rib in a roasting pan, uncovered.
6. Cook in oven, turning every 5 minutes, for 10-15 minutes in total.
7. Turn down the oven to 275° F, add 1 cup of hot water to the pan and cover with a lid.
8. Cook for 35-40 minutes until desired doneness is reached: 140-145° F for rare to medium-rare and 150-155° F for medium. To caramelize a bit, remove the lid for the last 10 minutes of the cooking time.
9. Remove roast from the oven and allow the meat to rest, covered, for 10 minutes.
10. Remove the cover and place roast on a cutting board. Cut in thin slices across the grain. Season with sea salt before serving.

Recipe Notes:

You can save the juices from the pan and simmer to create a thick sauce or use as a juice for dipping!

Ribeye Steak Sauté

Prep time: 10 minutes

Cooking time: 20 minutes

Servings: 1

Nutrients per serving:

Carbohydrates – 7 g

Fat – 70 g

Protein – 35 g

Calories – 798

Ingredients:

- 2 oz beef ribeye steak, sliced
- 1 tsp powdered onion
- 2 cloves garlic, minced
- 2 tbsp avocado oil, to cook with
- 1 sprig fresh parsley

Instructions:

1. To a frying pan on medium heat, add avocado oil and sauté the steak, garlic, and onion for about 20 minutes.
2. Top with parsley and enjoy!

Steak Au Poivre

Prep time: 5 minutes

Cooking time: 10 minutes

Servings: 1

Nutrients per serving:

Carbohydrates – 2 g

Fat – 58 g

Protein – 42 g

Calories – 696

Ingredients:

- 6 oz filet mignon, 1-inch thick
- 1 tbsp salt
- 2 tbsp peppercorns, crushed
- 1 sprig thyme
- 2 cloves garlic, crushed
- 2 tbsps ghee

Instructions:

1. Season the filet mignon with salt and let sit for 30 minutes.
2. Press the crushed peppercorns onto both sides of the filet mignon.
3. Add the garlic, ghee, and thyme to a hot skillet.
4. Add the steak when the ghee is hot and cook to desired doneness.

Seared Bacon Burgers

Prep time: 10 minutes

Cooking time: 20 minutes

Servings: 6

Nutrients per serving:

Carbohydrates – 7 g

Fat – 45 g

Protein – 22 g

Calories – 525

Ingredients:

- 4 oz bacon, diced
- 1½ lb ground beef
- ½ tsp salt
- ½ tsp black pepper

Instructions:

1. Cook the diced bacon in a frying pan until crispy.
2. Keep the bacon grease in the frying pan and combine the bacon bits with the raw ground beef. Season with salt and pepper. Form into 6 patties.
3. Fry the 6 burger patties on high heat, about 8-10 minutes per side.

Skillet Rib Eye Steaks

Prep time: 30 minutes (+2-3 days)

Cooking time: 25 minutes

Servings: 4

Nutrients per serving:

Carbohydrates – 0.2 g

Fat – 28 g

Protein – 22 g

Calories – 347

Ingredients:

- 1¼ lb bone-in rib-eye steaks (about 1¼-1½-inch thick)
- 1 tsp Stone House Seasoning
- 2 tbsps chopped fresh rosemary leaves
- 1 tbsp unsalted butter
- 1 tbsp olive oil

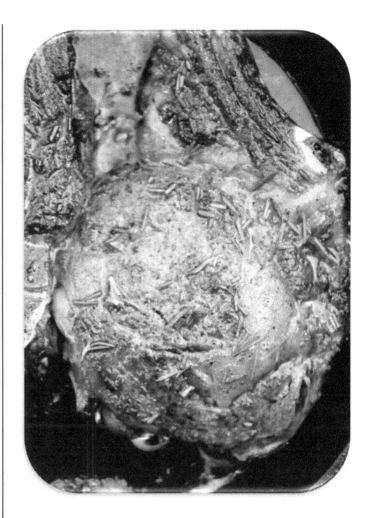

Instructions:

1. Rub both sides of steak with Stone House Seasoning.
2. Sprinkle with rosemary leaves.
3. Cover and refrigerate up to 3 days.
4. Remove from refrigerator and let rest at room temperature for 30 minutes.
5. Preheat a medium skillet over medium heat.
6. Add olive oil and butter and allow the butter to melt.
7. Place the steak into the skillet and cook about 5 minutes, until the bottom of the rib eye steak is caramelized and brown.
8. Turn the steak over and cook another 5 minutes, basting with the oil drippings from the skillet, until this side of the steak is also caramelized and brown.
9. Remove the steak from the heat on a cutting board and allow to rest for 5 minutes.
10. Slice against the grain when serving.

Roasted Beef Bone Marrow

Prep time: 5 minutes

Cooking time: 30 minutes

Servings: 2

Nutrients per serving:

Carbohydrates – 0 g

Fat – 48 g

Protein – 4 g

Calories – 440

Ingredients:

- 4 beef bone marrow halves
- A Pinch sea salt

Instructions:

1. Preheat oven to 350° F.
2. Place the bones on a baking tray; marrow side facing up.
3. Bake for 20-30 minutes until the bone and marrow are golden.

Herb Roasted Bone Marrow

Prep time: 5 minutes

Cooking time: 15 minutes

Servings: 2

Nutrients per serving:

Carbohydrates – 17.7 g

Fat – 1.6 g

Protein – 4 g

Calories – 113

Ingredients:

- 4 marrow beef bones
- ¼ tsp fresh rosemary, chopped
- ¼ tsp fresh thyme, chopped
- Salt and black pepper, to taste

Instructions:

1. Preheat the oven to 400° F.
2. Place the bones in a baking dish and sprinkle with rosemary and thyme.
3. Roast for about 15 minutes, until no longer pink inside.
4. Season with salt and pepper.
5. Serve hot.

WHITE MEAT

Chicken and Prosciutto Spiedini

Prep time: 15 minutes

Cooking time: 10 minutes

Servings: 8

Nutrients per serving:

Carbohydrates – 0.75 g

Fat – 10 g

Protein – 20 g

Calories – 174

Ingredients:

- 8 raw chicken tenders
- 8 oz block provolone cheese
- 8 slices prosciutto
- ½ tsp kosher salt
- ⅛ tsp ground black pepper
- 16 fresh basil leaves
- ¼ tsp garlic powder
- 8 skewers

Instructions:

1. Combine the garlic powder, kosher salt, and pepper.
2. Trim the chicken tenders of the tendons, and then pound them out to a half-inch thickness.
3. Season the chicken with the spice mixture.
4. Cut the provolone cheese into pieces about 1-2 inches long.
5. On a cutting board, place a slice of prosciutto. Then top with a chicken tender and two leaves of fresh basil. Next place a piece of cheese across the basil.
6. Carefully roll the bundle and skewer it.
7. Preheat a grill to 325-375°F. Grill for about 3-5 minutes per side, or until a thermometer reads 165°F in the center and the skewers are cooked through.
8. Serve warm.

Pinchos de Pollo Marinated Grilled Chicken Kebabs

Prep time: 10 minutes (+2 hours)

Cooking time: 10 minutes

Servings: 4

Nutrients per serving:

Carbohydrates – 3 g

Fat – 10 g

Protein – 39 g

Calories – 290

Ingredients:

- 1½ lb boneless, skinless chicken breast
- 1 tbsp minced garlic
- ½ tsp fine Himalayan salt
- ½ tsp freshly ground black pepper
- 1 tsp dried oregano
- 1 tbsp extra-virgin olive oil
- Juice of one lime
- 7-9 skewers

Instructions:

1. Have ready 7-9 soaked skewers.
2. In a bowl, combine the salt, garlic, pepper, lime juice, oregano, and oil.
3. Cut chicken breast into 1-inch chunks and place in a container with a lid.
4. Pour the marinade over the chicken and stir. Cover and refrigerate at least for 2 hours or overnight.

5. Preheat a grill to 325-375°F.
6. Remove the chicken from the refrigerator and thread onto the skewers, leaving a very small space between each piece and spreading each piece as flat as possible.
7. Once the grill is hot, grill the kebabs over direct medium heat, about 8-10 minutes total, keeping the lid closed until the chicken is no longer pink in the center and firm to the touch, turning once or twice during cooking. Take care not overcook.
8. Remove from the grill and serve immediately!

Slow Cooker Bacon and Chicken

Prep time: 5 minutes

Cooking time: 8 hours

Servings: 4

Nutrients per serving:

Carbohydrates – 3.6 g

Fat – 24 g

Protein – 22.9 g

Calories – 315

Ingredients:

- 5 chicken breasts
- 10 slices bacon
- 2 tbsp thyme, dried
- 1 tbsp oregano, dried
- 1 tbsp rosemary, dried
- 5 tbsp olive oil, divided
- 1 tbsp salt

Instructions:

1. Into a slow cooker pot, combine all the ingredients and two tablespoons of olive oil.
2. Cook on low for 8 hours.
3. Shred the meat and mix with remaining olive oil.

Garlic Bacon Wrapped Chicken Bites

Prep time: 10 minutes

Cooking time: 30 minutes

Servings: 4

Nutrients per serving:

Carbohydrates – 5.3 g

Fat – 5.9 g

Protein – 23.5 g

Calories – 170

Ingredients:

- 1 large skinless chicken breast, cut into small bites
- 9 slices bacon, cut into thirds
- 3 tbsp garlic powder

Instructions:

1. Preheat the oven to 400°F. Line a baking tray with foil.
2. Place the garlic powder in a bowl and dip each piece of chicken into the garlic powder.
3. Wrap each bacon piece around each garlic chicken bite.
4. Place each bite on the baking tray, spacing them out so that they're not touching.
5. Bake for 25-30 minutes until crispy.

Smokey Bacon Chicken Meatballs

Prep time: 15 minutes

Cooking time: 30 minutes

Servings: 8

Nutrients per serving:

Carbohydrates – 1 g

Fat – 25 g

Protein – 13 g

Calories – 280

Ingredients:

- 1 lb chicken breasts
- 8 slices bacon, cooked, crumbled
- 1 egg, whisked
- 2 cloves garlic
- 1 tbsp onion powder
- 2 drops liquid smoke
- 4 tbsps olive oil, to cook with
- 2 sprigs fresh parsley, to garnish

Instructions:

1. Into a food processor, place all the ingredients except the oil and mix well.
2. Form 20-24 small meatballs from the mixture.
3. Add the oil to a large frying pan, and allow to heat up.
4. Cook meatballs one side for 5 minutes until browned, then flip and cook on the other side for 5-10 minutes until done.
5. Serve immediately!

Asian Chicken Wings

Prep time: 10 minutes

Cooking time: 35 minutes

Servings: 5

Nutrients per serving:

Carbohydrates – 1 g

Fat – 22 g

Protein – 18 g

Calories – 277

Ingredients:

- 2 lbs chicken wings
- 2 tbsp sesame oil
- ¼ cup tamari sauce
- 1 tbsp ginger powder
- 2 tsp white wine vinegar
- 3 cloves garlic, minced
- ¼ tsp sea salt

Instructions:

1. Preheat oven to 400°F.
2. In a large container whisk together the ginger powder, sesame oil, salt, tamari sauce, vinegar, and garlic.
3. Add the wings to the mixture and stir to coat.
4. Place the wings on a lined baking sheet and bake for 30-35 minutes until golden and crispy.
5. If you want it crispier, turn on the broiler for a few minutes. Enjoy!

Baked Garlic Ghee Chicken Breast

Prep time: 5 minutes

Cooking time: 30 minutes

Servings: 1

Nutrients per serving:

Carbohydrates – 6.1 g

Fat – 15.5 g

Protein – 23.7 g

Calories – 264

Ingredients:

- 1 chicken breast
- 1 tsp garlic powder
- 1 tbsp ghee
- 2 cloves garlic, chopped
- 1 tsp sea salt
- 1 tsp chives, diced

Instructions:

1. Preheat oven to 350°F.
2. Place the chicken breast on a piece of foil.
3. Season with sea salt, garlic powder, chopped fresh garlic. Top with ghee and rub everything into the chicken breast.
4. Wrap the chicken breast in the foil and place on a baking tray.
5. Bake for 30 minutes, or until chicken breast is cooked through, with a meat thermometer reading above 165°F.
6. Serve with more salt and ghee to taste. Cut the chicken breast into slices and sprinkle diced chives on top.

Crispy Chicken Thighs

Prep time: 5 minutes

Cooking time: 40 minutes

Servings: 4

Nutrients per serving:

Carbohydrates – 0 g

Fat – 56 g

Protein – 48 g

Calories – 713

Ingredients:

- 12 chicken thighs
- 4 tbsps olive oil
- 2 tbsps salt
- 2 sprigs fresh rosemary, chopped

Instructions:

1. Preheat oven to 450° F.
2. Rub salt on each chicken thigh and place on a greased baking tray.
3. Drizzle the olive oil over the chicken thighs and top with the rosemary.
4. Bake for 40 minutes until golden and crispy. Enjoy!

Chicken and Bacon Sausages

Prep time: 10 minutes

Cooking time: 20 minutes

Servings: 12

Nutrients per serving:

Carbohydrates – 3 g

Fat – 21 g

Protein – 40 g

Calories – 370

Ingredients:

- 1 lb chicken breasts
- 2 slices bacon, cooked, crumbled
- 1 egg, whisked
- 2 tbsp Italian seasoning
- 2 tsp garlic powder
- 2 tsp onion powder
- ½ tsp salt
- ½ tsp pepper

Instructions:

1. Preheat the oven to 425° F.
2. Put all the ingredients into a food processor and process well.
3. From the meat mixture form approximately 12 thin patties (½-inch thick) and place on a baking tray lined with foil.
4. Bake for 20 minutes, until a meat thermometer shows 170° F.
5. Serve immediately or store in the freezer for 4 weeks.

Bifteck Hache (French Hamburgers)

Prep time: 15 minutes

Cooking time: 20 minutes

Servings: 4

Nutrients per serving:

Carbohydrates – 1 g

Fat – 36 g

Protein – 35 g

Calories – 460

Ingredients:

For the burgers:

- 1½ lb ground beef
- 4 tbsps ghee
- 1 onion, diced
- 1 egg
- 1 tbsp fresh thyme leaves
- ½ tsp salt
- ½ tsp pepper

For the sauce:

- ½ cup beef stock
- 2 tbsps ghee
- ¼ cup parsley, chopped

Instructions:

For the burgers:

1. Place 2 tbsps of ghee into a frying pan and cook half the diced onions until translucent, about 2-3 minutes.
2. Allow the onions to cool and add them with the oil in the pan to a mixing bowl with the egg, ground beef, salt, pepper, and thyme leaves.
3. Mix well and form 8 patties.
4. In a frying pan, cook the patties with 2 tbsps of ghee until both sides are well browned, about 5-6 minutes per side.

For the sauce:

5. Place the ghee into a frying pan and saute the remaining half of the onions, until translucent, about 2-3 minutes.
6. Add the beef stock and let cook until reduced, about 2-3 minutes. Add in the parsley.
7. Serve the sauce with the burgers.

Lemon Ghee Roast Chicken

Prep time: 10 minutes

Cooking time: 1 hour 45 minutes

Servings: 8

Nutrients per serving:

Carbohydrates – 0 g

Fat – 30 g

Protein – 43 g

Calories – 91432

Ingredients:

- 4 lb whole chicken, remove giblets
- 1 lemon, zested, sliced
- 1 lemon, halved
- ½ cup ghee
- 1 tbsp salt

Instructions:

1. Preheat the oven to 350° F.
2. Combine lemon zest and ½ tbsp salt and rub all over the chicken.
3. Sprinkle ½ tbsp salt into the chicken cavity and stuff with lemon halves and ¼ cup of ghee.
4. Brush the remaining ghee on the outside of the chicken.
5. Place the chicken in a roasting pan and arrange the lemon slices around the chicken.
6. Roast for 1 hour 45 minutes. Using a meat thermometer, cook until the internal temperature of the meat is 165°F.
7. Let the chicken rest for about 10 minutes before slicing and serving.

Oven-Baked Parmesan Garlic Wings

Prep time: 5 minutes

Cooking time: 30 minutes

Servings: 12

Nutrients per serving:

Carbohydrates –0.6 g

Fat – 45.9 g

Protein –45.4 g

Calories – 602

Ingredients:

- 6 lbs whole chicken wings
- 8 tbsp butter, melted
- 1 egg
- ½ tsp Italian seasoning
- ½ cup Parmesan cheese
- 1 tsp garlic powder
- ¼ tsp crushed red pepper
- ¼ tsp salt

Instructions:

1. Preheat the oven to 425° F. Cut the wings into two sections.
2. Put the wings on a baking sheet with a metal rack on top. Cook for 15 minutes.
3. Make the sauce by by combining the cheese, butter, seasonings, and egg in a small bowl. Don't worry about using a raw egg in the sauce; the wings will be hot enough.
4. Remove the wings from the oven and flip them over. Turn on the broiler and broil for 5 minutes. Flip again and broil for another 5 minutes. Keep flipping and broiling until they are done to your desired crispness. They should reach an internal temperature of 165°F.
5. Toss immediately in the sauce.
6. Garnish with extra cheese.

Crispy Indian Chicken Drumsticks

Prep time: 5 minutes

Cooking time: 40 minutes

Servings: 5

Nutrients per serving:

Carbohydrates – 3.6 g

Fat – 24.3 g

Protein – 34.7 g

Calories – 362

Ingredients:

- 2 lbs chicken drumsticks
- 2 tbsps salt
- 3 tbsp garam masala
- ½ tbsp coconut oil

Instructions:

1. Preheat the oven to 450° F
2. Smear a large baking tray with coconut oil.
3. In a bowl, mix the garam masala and salt.
4. Pat the drumsticks dry.
5. Coat each drumstick with the mixture and lay on the baking tray.
6. Bake for 40 minutes. Serve immediately.

Whole Roast Chicken

Prep time: 15 minutes

Cooking time: 1 hour 30 minutes

Servings: 8

Nutrients per serving:

Carbohydrates – 0.4 g

Fat – 13.7 g

Protein – 29.3 g

Calories – 243

Ingredients:

- 3 lbs whole organic chicken
- 2 sprigs fresh rosemary
- 2 garlic cloves
- 1 tsp Herbes de Provence
- 1 tbsp coarse sea salt

Instructions:

1. Preheat oven to 350°F.
2. Rinse the chicken well under cold water.
3. Place chicken on a baking pan, breast up.
4. Stuff the cavity with the garlic cloves and rosemary.
5. Mix the salt and Herbes the Provence in a small bowl. Sprinkle half of the mixture on the breast.
6. Turn chicken breast side down and sprinkle the remaining mixture on the top.
7. Bake for 1 hour 30 minutes, until the chicken skin is nicely browned.
8. Serve immediately.

Duck Leg Confit

Prep time: 15 minutes (+12 hours)

Cooking time: 2hours 30 minutes

Servings: 4

Nutrients per serving:

Carbohydrates – 3.5 g

Fat – 66 g

Protein – 18.9 g

Calories – 688

Ingredients:

- 4 duck legs with thighs attached, excess duck fat trimmed and reserved
- 1 tbsp + ¼ tsp kosher salt
- ½ tsp table salt
- ½ tsp black pepper
- 10 garlic cloves
- 4 bay leaves
- 4 sprigs fresh thyme
- 1½ tsp black peppercorns
- 4 cups olive oil

Instructions:

1. Put the reserved duck fat in the bottom of a plastic or glass container.
2. On a platter, lay two duck legs, skin side down. Season with black pepper, 1 tbsp kosher salt, thyme, garlic cloves, and bay leaves.
3. Lay the remaining two duck legs on top, flesh to flesh. Sprinkle with the remaining ¼ tsp kosher salt. Cover and refrigerate for 12 hours.
4. Preheat the oven to 300°F.
5. Remove duck legs from the fridge.
6. Remove and reserve the thyme, garlic, bay leaves, and duck fat. Rinse the duck legs with cold water, rubbing off some of the pepper and salt. Pat dry with paper towels.
7. In the bottom of an enamel cast iron pot, put the reserved bay leaves, garlic, duck fat, and thyme. Sprinkle with the salt and peppercorns.
8. Lay the duck legs in the pot, skin side down, and add the olive oil.
9. Cover and bake for 2.5-3 hours, or until the meat pulls away from the bone.
10. Remove the duck from the fat. Strain the fat and reserve.
11. In a hot pan, sear duck legs skin-side down until the skin is crispy and golden, about 3-4 minutes. Serve immediately.

Recipe Notes:

To save for later, pick the meat from the bones and place it in a container. Cover the duck with a ¼ -inch layer of strained fat. The confit can be stored in the refrigerator for up to one month.

Turkey Meatballs

Prep time: 10 minutes

Cooking time: 30 minutes

Servings: 6

Nutrients per serving:

Carbohydrates – 2 g

Fat – 16 g

Protein – 28.8 g

Calories – 274

Ingredients:

- ¾ cup milk
- ⅓ cup crushed pork rinds
- 1 large egg
- 1 tsp salt
- ½ tsp freshly ground black pepper
- ¾ cup Parmesan cheese, grated
- 1 tbsp dried parsley
- 1 ¼ lb turkey, minced
- 1 tbsp dried minced onion
- 1 clove garlic, finely minced

Instructions:

1. Combine all ingredients together in a large bowl.
2. Using large scoop, form mixture into even-sized balls and place on a baking sheet.
3. Preheat the oven to 400°F and bake for 25-30 minutes.

Turkey Scotch Eggs

Prep time: 15 minutes

Cooking time: 32 minutes

Servings: 6

Nutrients per serving:

Carbohydrates – 1 g

Fat – 13 g

Protein – 24 g

Calories – 241

Ingredients:

- 6 hard-boiled eggs, cooled, peeled, dry
- 1 lb ground turkey
- 1 egg
- 2 tsp garlic powder
- 1 tsp poultry seasoning
- ½ tbsp Cajun seasoning

Grain-Free Breading:

- ¼ cup Parmesan cheese
- ½ tsp salt
- ½ tsp black pepper

Instructions:

1. Preheat the oven to 400° F.
2. In a bowl, combine the turkey, garlic powder, poultry seasoning, and Cajun seasoning. Mix well. Make 6 patties.
3. Beat an egg in a separate bowl.
4. In another bowl, mix the grain-free breading ingredients.
5. Place hard-boiled egg on a patty, and roll in hands around the egg until covered and ball-shaped.
6. Dip and roll in egg, then roll in cheese mixture till covered.
7. Place on a parchment-lined casserole baking dish.
8. Bake for 30 minutes. Then broil on low for 2-3 minutes, just until browned.
9. Serve immediately.

Roasted Paprica Turkey Wings

Prep time: 10 minutes

Cooking time: 45 minutes

Servings: 4

Nutrients per serving:

Carbohydrates – 0 g

Fat – 24 g

Protein – 34 g

Calories – 370

Ingredients:

- 15 lb turkey wings
- 1 tbs olive oil
- Salt and pepper, to taste
- 1 tsp paprika

Instructions:

1. Preheat the oven to 375° F. Line a baking pan with foil, and place a metal rack on top.
2. Remove the wingtips and any excess fat or skin.
3. Place the wings on the rack and drizzle with olive oil, then season with salt and pepper.
4. Roast until the wings are cooked, about 40 minutes. During the last five minutes of cooking, sprinkle paprika over the wings and return to the oven.

FISH and SEAFOOD

Lemon Baked Salmon

Prep time: 5 minutes

Cooking time: 20 minutes

Servings: 2

Nutrients per serving:

Carbohydrates – 2 g

Fat – 44 g

Protein – 42 g

Calories – 571

Ingredients:

- 12 oz filets of salmon
- 2 lemons, sliced thinly
- 2 tbsps olive oil
- Salt and black pepper, to taste
- 3 sprigs thyme

Instructions:

1. Preheat the oven to 350° F.
2. Place half the sliced lemons on the bottom of a baking dish. Place the fillets over the lemons and cover with the remaining lemon slices and thyme.
3. Drizzle olive oil over the dish and cook for 20 minutes.
4. Season with salt and pepper.

Easy Blackened Shrimp

Prep time: 10 minutes

Cooking time: 6 minutes

Servings: 2

Nutrients per serving:

Carbohydrates – 5.1 g

Fat – 3.9 g

Protein – 24.4 g

Calories – 152

Ingredients:

- ½ lb shrimp, peeled and deveined
- 2 tbsp blackened seasoning
- 1 tsp olive oil
- Juice of 1 lemon

Instructions:

1. Toss all ingredients (except oil) together until shrimp are well coated.
2. In a non-stick skillet, heat the oil to medium-high heat.
3. Add shrimp and cook 2-3 minutes per side.
4. Serve immediately.

Grilled Shrimp Easy Seasoning

Prep time: 5 minutes

Cooking time: 5 minutes

Servings: 4

Nutrients per serving:

Carbohydrates – 1 g

Fat – 3 g

Protein – 28 g

Calories – 102

Ingredients:

For the shrimp seasoning:

- 1 tsp garlic powder
- 1 tsp kosher salt
- 1 tsp Italian seasoning
- ¼ tsp cayenne pepper

For grilling:

- 2 tbsps olive oil
- 1 tbsp lemon juice
- 1 lb jumbo shrimp, peeled, deveined
- Ghee for the grill

Instructions:

1. Preheat the grill pan to high.
2. In a mixing bowl, stir together the seasoning ingredients.
3. Drizzle in the lemon juice and olive oil and stir.
4. Add the shrimp and toss to coat.
5. Brush the grill pan with ghee.
6. Grill the shrimp until pink, about 2-3 minutes per side.
7. Serve immediately.

The Best Garlic Cilantro Salmon

Prep time: 10 minutes

Cooking time: 15 minutes

Servings: 4

Nutrients per serving:

Carbohydrates – 3.5 g

Fat – 4 g

Protein – 24.9 g

Calories – 140

Ingredients:

- 1 lb salmon filet
- 1 tbsp butter
- 1 lemon
- ¼ cup fresh cilantro leaves, chopped
- 4 cloves garlic, minced
- ½ tsp Kosher salt
- ½ tsp freshly cracked black pepper

Instructions:

1. Preheat oven to 400° F.
2. On a foil-lined baking sheet, place salmon skin side down.
3. Squeeze lemon over the salmon.
4. Season salmon with cilantro and garlic, pepper and salt.
5. Slice butter thinly and place pieces evenly over the salmon.
6. Bake for about 7 minutes, depending on thickness.
7. Turn the oven to broil and cook 5-7 minutes, until the top is crispy.
8. Remove salmon from oven and serve immediately.

Crispy Oven Roasted Salmon

Prep time: 5 minutes

Cooking time: 20 minutes

Servings: 3

Nutrients per serving:

Carbohydrates – 0.2 g

Fat – 28.7 g

Protein – 35.8 g

Calories – 400

Ingredients:

- 1 lb salmon fillet
- ¼ tsp sea salt
- 2 tbsp coconut oil
- ½ tsp mixed herbs (oregano, thyme, marjoram)

Instructions:

1. Preheat the oven to 425° F. Line a baking sheet with parchment paper and grease with one tablespoon of coconut oil.
2. Place the fillet on the lined baking sheet skin side down.
3. Season with salt and herbs.
4. Place one tablespoon of coconut oil on top of the salmon.
5. Cook for 20 minutes or until your desired level of crispiness is reached.
6. Serve immediately.

Recipe Notes:

You can store the dish in a glass container in the fridge for up to 2 days.

Aromatic Dover Sole Fillets

Prep time: 5 minutes

Cooking time: 20 minutes

Servings: 2

Nutrients per serving:

Carbohydrates – 2.9 g

Fat – 17.9 g

Protein – 18.6 g

Calories – 244

Ingredients:

- 6 Dover Sole fillets
- ¼ cup virgin olive oil
- Zest of 1 lemon
- Dash of cardamom powder
- 1 cup fresh cilantro leaves
- Pinch of sea salt

Instructions:

1. Bring the fillets to room temperature.
2. Set the oven's broiler to high.
3. Pour half of the oil in an oven tray.
4. Add half of the cilantro leaves, half of the lemon zest, and the cardamom powder.
5. Lay the fillets in the mixture and top with the remaining ingredients.
6. Set under the broiler for about 7-8 minutes or until the fish breaks easily with a fork and it is not transparent.
7. Serve immediately.

Bacon-Wrapped Salmon

Prep time: 10 minutes

Cooking time: 20 minutes

Servings: 2

Nutrients per serving:

Carbohydrates – 7.1 g

Fat –42 g

Protein – 53.3 g

Calories – 612

Ingredients:

- 2 salmon fillets
- 1 tbsp olive oil
- 4 slices bacon
- Lemon wedges
- 2 tbsp tarragon

Instructions:

1. Preheat the oven to 350°F.
2. Pat the filets dry.
3. Wrap bacon around the salmon filets.
4. Place filets on a roasting tray, and drizzle with the olive oil.
5. Bake for 15-20 minutes.
6. Garnish with lemon wedges and chopped tarragon.

Japanese Fish Bone Broth

Prep time: 5 minutes

Cooking time: 4 hours

Servings: 6-8

Nutrients per serving:

Carbohydrates – 0 g

Fat – 2 g

Protein – 5 g

Calories – 40

Ingredients:

- Fish head and carcass
- 4 slices ginger
- 1 tbsp lemon juice
- ½ leek, sliced
- Sea salt, to taste
- Water

Instructions:

1. Place the fish head and carcass into a large pot with cold water.
2. Bring to a boil and pour out the water.
3. Refill the pot with fresh water and add in the leek, sea salt, ginger, and lemon juice.
4. Simmer, covered, about 4 hours.

Garlic Ghee Pan-Fried Cod

Prep time: 5 minutes

Cooking time: 10 minutes

Servings: 4

Nutrients per serving:

Carbohydrates – 1 g

Fat – 7 g

Protein – 21 g

Calories – 160

Ingredients:

- 1¼ lb cod fillets
- 3 tbsps ghee
- 6 cloves of garlic, minced
- 1 tbsp garlic powder
- A pinch salt

Instructions:

1. In a frying pan on medium-high heat, melt the ghee.
2. Add half the minced garlic.
3. Place the cod fillets in the pan and sprinkle with garlic powder and salt.
4. Cook until fish is a solid white color, about 4-5 minutes. Then flip the fillets and add the remaining minced garlic. Cook until the whole fillets turn a solid white color, about 4-5 minutes.
5. Serve with the ghee and garlic from the pan.

Steam Your Own Lobster

Prep time: 10 minutes

Cooking time: 10 minutes

Servings: 4

Nutrients per serving:

Carbohydrates – 0 g

Fat – 0 g

Protein – 24 g

Calories – 100

Ingredients:

- 4 lobster tails
- 1 sprig parsley

Instructions:

1. If the lobster tails are frozen, defrost them.
2. Before cooking, make a long slit in the underbelly of the lobster.
3. Fill a pot halfway with water. Place a steamer basket inside.
4. Once the water is boiling, place the lobster tails onto the steamer attachment.
5. Let boil for for 8-9 minutes for fresh lobster and 10 minutes for defrosted lobster.
6. Garnish with parsley.

Recipe Notes:

If using fresh lobster, steam it for 8-9 minutes.

Thyme Roasted Salmon

Prep time: 10 minutes

Cooking time: 20 minutes

Servings: 4

Nutrients per serving:

Carbohydrates – 0 g

Fat – 9 g

Protein – 25 g

Calories – 186

Ingredients:

- 1 lb fresh salmon, skinless
- 2 tsp olive oil
- ¼ tsp kosher salt
- 1 tbsp ghee
- ½ tsp dried thyme
- Lemon wedges

Instructions:

1. Preheat oven to 400° F.
2. Cut salmon into four equal-sized pieces.
3. Line a sheet pan with parchment paper and place salmon on it.
4. Brush with olive oil and season with salt.
5. Roast for 10 minutes.
6. In a small bowl, mix dried thyme and ghee. Set aside.
7. After 10 minutes of cooking, brush salmon with thyme-ghee mixture.
8. Roast for 5-8 minutes more, or until salmon is just cooked through.
9. Before serving, allow to rest for 10 minutes.

Pan-Fried Tilapia

Prep time: 10 minutes

Cooking time: 10 minutes

Servings: 4

Nutrients per serving:

Carbohydrates – 0.7 g

Fat – 1 g

Protein – 21 g

Calories – 91

Ingredients:

- 2 tilapia filets
- Salt, to taste
- 2 tbsps coconut oil

Instructions:

1. Add coconut oil to a frying pan on medium heat.
2. Salt the tilapia fillets.
3. Place the fillets in the frying pan and cook until fish is a solid white color, about 4-5 minutes. Then flip the fillets and cook until the whole fillets turn a solid white color, about 4-5 minutes.
4. Serve immediately.

Calamari Rings

Prep time: 5 minutes

Cooking time: 2 minutes

Servings: 4

Nutrients per serving:

Carbohydrates – 5.9 g

Fat – 8.2 g

Protein – 16.3 g

Calories – 159

Ingredients:

- 4 calamari squid tubes
- 1 tbsp ghee
- 2 tbsp almond flour
- Zest and juice of 1 lemon
- Salt and pepper, to taste

Instructions:

1. Mix the almond flour, lemon zest, salt, and pepper.
2. Slice the squid tubes into ½-inch slices.
3. Roll the calamari rings in the almond mix.
4. Heat ghee in a frying pan and fry rings on low heat for 1 minute each side until cooked and golden.
5. Drizzle with lemon juice.

ORGAN MEAT

Pan-Seared Beef Tongue

Prep time: 10 minutes

Cooking time: 70 minutes

Servings: 3

Nutrients per serving:

Carbohydrates – 0 g

Fat – 39 g

Protein – 22 g

Calories – 448

Ingredients:

- 12 oz whole beef tongue
- 3 cups water
- 1 tbsp olive oil
- Salt and black pepper, to taste

Instructions:

1. Wash tongue under cold water.
2. Place tongue and water in a pressure cooker.
3. Cook on the "stew" setting for 35 minutes.
4. Let pressure release naturally, about 30 minutes.
5. Remove from pressure cooker and peel skin from the tongue skinless.
6. Cut the tongue into 1-inch medallions.
7. Season with salt and pepper.
8. Sear in a frying pan with olive oil, about 2-3 minutes per side.

Recipe Notes:

You can do this with a large pot or a slow cooker. Simply boil, then simmer on low heat for about 1 hour.

Liver Bacon Meatballs

Prep time: 20 minutes (+24 hours)

Cooking time: 15 minutes

Servings: 8

Nutrients per serving:

Carbohydrates – 2.4 g

Fat – 32.9 g

Protein – 32.1 g

Calories – 441

Ingredients:

- 1½ lbs ground beef
- ½ lb beef liver
- 8 oz bacon, diced
- 1 egg
- 1 shallot, finely chopped
- 1 pinch cayenne pepper
- ¼ cup full-fat coconut oil
- ½ tsp sea salt
- ½ tsp freshly ground black pepper
- 2 tbsps apple cider vinegar

Instructions:

1. Rinse the beef liver under cold water to wash out all the blood traces. Pat dry with paper towels.
2. Remove all tough veins using a sharp knife.
3. Marinate liver in apple cider vinegar for 24 hours in the refrigerator.
4. Remove from marinade and pat dry.
5. Cook bacon over low heat in a large pan, stirring, about 5 minutes, without being too crispy.

6. Place the bacon on a plate covered with a paper towel, reserving the rendered lard in the pan.
7. Whisk the egg lightly with the coconut cream, a pinch of freshly ground black pepper and a pinch of sea salt.
8. In a food processor, add the liver and process about 2-3 minutes, until it almost turns liquid.
9. Add the beef, bacon, egg mixture, shallot, cayenne, the remaining sea salt, and pepper.
10. Blend very lightly, just until combined.
11. Form the meat mixture into golfball-sized meatballs.
12. Put the meatballs in the pan over medium heat and brown on both sides, about 2-3 minutes per side.
13. Cover the saucepan and let the meatballs cook for about 10 minutes on a low flame.

Beef Heart Steak

Prep time: 10 minutes (+24 hours)

Cooking time: 10 minutes

Servings: 4

Nutrients per serving:

Carbohydrates – 0.2 g

Fat – 13.3 g

Protein – 23 g

Calories – 213

Ingredients:

- 4 slices beef heart, 1-inch thick
- 1 tbsp ghee
- 2 tbsps olive oil
- 1 tsp rosemary
- Salt and pepper, to taste
- ¼ cup apple cider vinegar

Instructions:

1. Marinate heart slices in apple cider vinegar for 24 hours in the refrigerator.
2. Remove from the marinade and pat dry.
3. In a cast-iron skillet over high heat, add the ghee and let melt for 40 seconds.
4. Lay heart slices in the skillet and cook for 5 minutes on each side until nicely browned, but still pink in the middle.
5. Drizzle with the olive oil.

Slow-Cooked Chicken Gizzard

Prep time: 10 minutes

Cooking time: 6 hours

Servings: 2

Nutrients per serving:

Carbohydrates – 7.2 g

Fat – 2.4 g

Protein – 21.8 g

Calories – 157

Ingredients:

- 1 lb chicken gizzards
- 1 bunch cilantro, washed, cleaned from stems
- 3 large cloves garlic, peeled, sliced
- 1 small onion
- ¼ cup Passata di Pomodoro
- ½ cup white table wine
- ¼ cup water
- ½ tsp Celtic sea salt

Instructions:

1. In the slow cooker, add all the ingredients and mix well, so the chicken gizzards are partially submerged.
2. Cook for 6 hours on low.

Grilled Beef Liver Steak

Prep time: 10 minutes (+24 hours)

Cooking time: 15 minutes

Servings: 5

Nutrients per serving:

Carbohydrates – 4 g

Fat – 25 g

Protein – 19 g

Calories – 315

Ingredients:

- 1 lb beef liver, cut into 1-inch slices
- ½ cup olive oil
- 1 clove garlic, crushed
- 1 tbsp fresh mint, chopped
- ¼ tsp black pepper
- 1 tsp salt
- ¼ cup apple cider vinegar

Instructions:

1. Rinse the beef liver under cold water to wash out all the blood traces. Pat dry with paper towels.
2. Remove all tough veins using a sharp knife.
3. Marinate liver slices in apple cider vinegar for 24 hours in the refrigerator.
4. Remove slices from the marinade and pat dry.
5. Preheat a grill pan over medium-high heat.
6. In a small bowl, combine mint, olive oil, crushed garlic, salt, and pepper until well mixed.
7. Lay the liver slices on a grill pan and generously brush them with the spice mixture.
8. Grill for 5-7 minutes on each side.
9. Enjoy!

Bacon-Wrapped Chicken Liver with Sage

Prep time: 15 minutes

Cooking time: 20 minutes

Servings: 4

Nutrients per serving:

Carbohydrates – 8.3 g

Fat – 38.9 g

Protein – 31.2 g

Calories – 484

Ingredients:

- 1lb bacon
- 1 lb chicken livers
- 1 package fresh sage
- 9-10 skewers

Instructions:

1. Preheat oven to 450°F.
2. Clean the livers from excess fat and veins.
3. Wash and dry the livers thoroughly, then cut into bite-sized pieces.
4. Cut bacon strips in half.
5. Place one piece of liver and one piece of sage on bacon and roll. Stick onto a skewer, making sure there's some space in between each to cook well.
6. Bake for 20-25 minutes, until crispy and brown. Drain on paper towels.
7. Garnish with fresh sage and eat while warm.

Chicken Liver with Raw Garlic and Thyme

Prep time: 10 minutes

Cooking time: 7 minutes

Servings: 4

Nutrients per serving:

Carbohydrates – 3.2 g

Fat – 16 g

Protein – 19.4 g

Calories – 229

Ingredients:

- 1 lb chicken liver, thinly sliced
- 3 tbsp extra-virgin olive oil
- Juice of 1 lemon
- 4 cloves garlic, minced
- ½ tsp sea salt
- 5 sprigs fresh thyme
- 2 tbsp ghee to fry

Instructions:

1. Clean the livers from excess fat and veins.
2. Wash and dry the livers thoroughly.
3. Heat ghee in a skillet on medium-high and fry the livers for 3-4 minutes on one side; and 2-3 minutes on the other side , until no longer pink inside.
4. Remove from the pan and coat with garlic, olive oil, thyme, and sea salt.
5. Enjoy!

BBQ Chicken Livers

Prep time: 10 minutes

Cooking time: 10 minutes

Servings: 2

Nutrients per serving:

Carbohydrates – 2 g

Fat – 10.8 g

Protein – 38.1 g

Calories – 262

Ingredients:

- 1 lb chicken livers
- ½ tsp sea salt
- ½ black pepper

Instructions:

1. Clean the livers from excess fat and veins.
2. Heat grill to medium-high.
3. Lay livers flat on a grilling basket.
4. Season with freshly ground black pepper and sea salt.
5. Set on the grill and cook about 10 minutes, turning halfway through.

BBQ Chicken Hearts

Prep time: 10 minutes

Cooking time: 20 minutes

Servings: 2

Nutrients per serving:

Carbohydrates – 1.9 g

Fat – 21 g

Protein – 35.1 g

Calories – 346

Ingredients

- 1 lb chicken hearts
- ½ tsp sea salt
- ½ black pepper
- 3 skewers

Instructions:

1. Clean the hearts from excess fat and veins.
2. With a sharp knife, remove the heart's tough top parts.
3. Heat grill to medium-high.
4. Thread the hearts on the skewers, 5-7 on each.
5. Season hearts with freshly ground black pepper and sea salt.
6. Grill about 15-20 minutes, turning halfway through.
7. Serve immediately.

CONCLUSION

Thank you for reading this book and having the patience to try the recipes.

I do hope that you have had as much enjoyment reading and experimenting with the meals as I have had writing the book.

If you would like to leave a comment, you can do so at the Order section->Digital orders, in your account.

Stay safe and healthy!

Recipe Index

Conversion Tables

VOLUME EQUIVALENTS (LIQUID)

US STANDARD	US STANDARD (OUNCES)	METRIC
2 tablespoons	1 fl. oz.	30 mL
¼ cup	2 fl. oz.	60 mL
½ cup	4 fl. oz.	120 mL
1 cup	8 fl. oz.	240mL
1½ cups	12 fl. oz.	355 mL
2 cups or 1 pint	16 fl. oz.	475 mL
4 cups or 1 quart	32 fl. oz.	1 L
1 gallon	128 fl. oz.	4 L

OVEN TEMPERATURES

FAHRENHEIT (°F)	CELSIUS (°C) APPROXIMATE
250 °F	120 °C
300 °F	150 °C
325 °F	165 °C
350 °F	180 °C
375 °F	190 °C
400 °F	200 °C
425 °F	220 °C
450 °F	230 °C

VOLUME EQUIVALENTS (LIQUID)

US STANDARD	METRIC (APPROXIMATE)
1/8 teaspoon	0.5 mL
¼ teaspoon	1 mL
½ teaspoon	2 mL
2/3 teaspoon	4 mL
1 teaspoon	5 mL
1 tablespoon	15 mL
¼ cup	59 mL
1/3 cup	79 mL
½ cup	118 mL
2/3 cup	156 mL
¾ cup	177 mL
1 cup	235 mL
2 cups or 1 pint	475 mL
3 cups	700 mL
4 cups or 1 quart	1 L
½ gallon	2 L
1 gallon	4 L

WEIGHT EQUIVALENTS

US STANDARD	METRIC (APPROXIMATE)
½ ounce	15 g
1 ounce	30 g
2 ounces	60 g
4 ounces	115 g
8 ounces	225 g
12 ounces	340 g
16 ounces or 1 pound	455 g

Other Books by Kaitlyn Donnelly